WALKS IN BUCKINGHAMSHIRE

Walks in Buckinghamshire

VERA BURDEN

SPURBOOKS LIMITED

Published by
SPURBOOKS LIMITED
6 Parade Court
Bourne End
Buckinghamshire

© VERA BURDEN 1978

At the time of publication all footpaths used in these walks were designated as official footpaths, but it should be borne in mind that diversion orders may be made from time to time.

Although every care has been taken in the preparation of this Guide, neither the Author, nor the Publisher can accept responsibility for those who stray from the Rights of Way.

ISBN 0 904978 81 8

Printed by Maund & Irvine Ltd., Tring, Herts.

Contents

ACKNOWLEDGEMENTS

Acknowledgement is made to the Bucks Examiner for kindly allowing the use of some material previously printed by them, and to the efforts of the Chiltern Society and other Rambling groups.

Introduction

In compiling this book of walks I have chosen as varied a selection as possible. Having the Chiltern hills, an Area of Outstanding Natural Beauty, in the south, Buckinghamshire is a county well endowed with footpaths.

Each route, whether it climbs the chalk escarpments, follows the woodland rides, the level meadow paths, or the ancient tracks linking one settlement with another, has its own attraction. One path may meet a solitary farm, a pub, a village, another give glimpses of a stately home, encounter a Norman, even a Saxon church, as at Wing, or pass signs of prehistoric man in the form of the remains of a hill-fort or a well preserved stretch of Grim's Ditch, as at Hampden. Wherever you walk, especially if you make your way quietly, you never know what wildlife you may see. To go on foot is the only way of really getting to know, to understand and to appreciate the English countryside.

The Chiltern tracks are, in general, more obvious and more used than those crossing the less populated pastoral land to the north. Although none of the routes exceeds 5 miles, some are a little more strenuous than others. Where the going is rather heavier underfoot it is indicated in the text.

The footpaths are here for our use and enjoyment, but just as the Highway Code is meant to safeguard the motorist and the pedestrian, so the Countryside Code has been drawn up to protect the rights of both landowner and walker. So please be careful to close all gates after use and to abide by the rights of way.

V.B.

ABBREVIATIONS

P.F. Public Footpath
P.F. and B. Public Footpath and Bridleway
W.A. White Arrow (Waymark)

WALK 1
HAMBLEDEN
DAIRY LANE, GREAT WOOD, BACRES FARM.
5 Miles

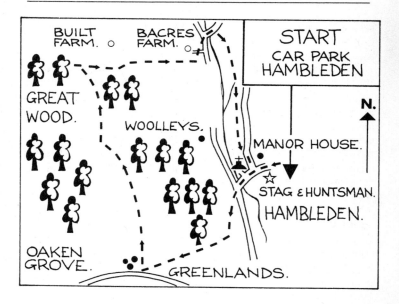

An infinitely rewarding walk, whatever the time of year. Travelling through meadowland and beechwoods around and above the Hambleden Valley, there are impressive views from the higher paths, whilst those on the floor of the valley are wonderfully secluded. Look out for pheasant, partridge, lapwing and all the wayside and woodland birds.

How to get there. By car to Hambleden village car park (free).

Leaving the village car park behind the *Stag and Huntsman,* go left to pass the pub, the church and the village post office in that order. Then on, over the bridge crossing the bed of the Hamble, where ignore P.F. left and walk on to road junction.

8

Cross and go between posts to follow P.F. & B. going up to quickly pass the school. When path ceases to be surfaced, carry on up, staying with main path to soon pass a group of posts. Then, at fork, take lower left-hand track. Keep ahead, disregarding all diversions, to find that the ground levels.

Already there is much to catch the eye, with a richly variegated hedgerow developing right, and brief glimpses of the Thames, like polished steel, to the left.

On arrival at surfaced way — Dairy Lane — turn right along it to pass a pair of estate cottages, dated 1876. It is now, by means of a wide 5-bar gate, that you enter the Greenlands estate, a wide acreage protected by the National Trust.

If you have a dog with you, please keep it under control. A score or more pheasants may be flushed up as you follow the broad, stony track lying in the hollow of the hills, with farmland sweeping up to the left.

All turnings off are to be disregarded. On arrival at a crossing track and gate continue forward, shortly to regain the shade of overhanging trees. At division of track, use right forward fork. Climbing gradually, the land falling away to left has been overtaken by the rampant willow herb.

When the beeches of Great Wood are reached, you immediately meet a gathering of ways, where you should see a white footpath sign on a trunk before you. Turn sharp right up obvious track. Uphill again here, and the numerous side paths — all to be avoided — account for the very explicit directions over the next short distance.

Soon larch saplings appear left, and on this plantation ending, at a T-junction of paths, go left for 100 yards to a further crossing track. Here keep to your wide track as it curves right and down. Just 80 yards on again ignore paths to left and right and carry on forward. Sharply downhill now, and when path joins from left still go ahead as track soon becomes surfaced.

The houses of Colstrope will come into view away left, and at the bottom swing left to pass by a brick and flint wall of Bacres farm. Go on past the farmhouse, and, ignoring drive right, walk via a wooden gate facing you into meadow. Probably there is no sign of path here, but just go diagonally across corner of meadow using house seen ahead as your goal. At far side come out through metal gate to road and a reassuring P.F. sign.

Cross road and go down road towards Colstrope. After 70 yards having re-crossed the bed of the Hamble, turn right over stile to follow P.F. diagonally left. A few yards on cross a stile to maintain direction to next waymarked stile in opposite hedge. Beyond it go sharp right, thus keeping hedge on right for 50 yards then it appears on left.

Walk on and through two kissing-gates to pass beside house and arrive at a concrete driveway. Still forward as the path, marked by a series of gates, travels between houses and gardens, and as they cease, goes via a kissing-gate and on over grass. A couple more similar gates usher you through a narrow belt of trees and ahead, now parallel with the road from Pheasants Hill. Ignore stile left, to soon come upon yet a further gate, and at next stile, also left, climb over it — with appropriate care — to road.

A right turn and a few more steps will return you to Hambleden passing, as you go, the 17th-century gabled Manor house with its handsome copper beech, and the church. Amongst its numerous treasures are a nave altar famed for being constructed from a 15th-century bedhead used by Cardinal Wolsey; a Lady Chapel window showing a likeness of St. Thomas de Canteloupe, Hambleden's most eminent son; and an endearing alabaster monument of Sir Cope D'Oyley and his family.

Refreshments. *Stag and Huntsman* in village.

WALK 2

TURVILLE HEATH
Turville Court, Turville Valley Farm,
Turville Grange
4 Miles

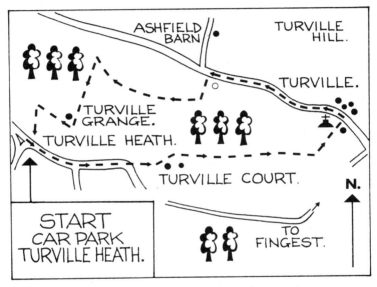

Once off the heath, a popular summertime rendezvous, you are as likely to see a deer fleeting through the trees as to meet another human being on these enchanting wooded tracks. In the lanes the most familiar sight hereabouts is a string of ponies being exercised by young horsewomen. Be prepared for a short, sharp climb on the way back.

A minor diversion will take you into Turville, a timeless village of exceptional charm, where the small Norman church, the picturesque *Bull and Butcher* and an array of period cottages cluster around the miniature green.

How to get there. By car to Turville Heath.

The setting off point is the junction of minor roads at Turville Heath; one to Stonor and Henley, one to Northend and Watlington and the third to Turville. Also note a P.F. & B. sign pointing across the heath. Use as a landmark only, and start off along the road to Turville, thus soon leaving Turville Grange, glimpsed across the heath, behind you.

Stay with road, passing several attractive cottages. After about 300 yards ignore road right to Southend and go on, ignoring all paths off. When road turns abruptly right and down, abandon it to go forward on *No Through Road* to Turville Court. As expected the road ends at the house, so turn left as P.F. & B. sign shows, and then keep on down lane for some 60 yards to enter wood.

(These sylvan paths in Churchfield Wood are liberally scattered with helpful waymarks, directing the pedestrian in varying directions. So to avoid confusion I will give rather precise details for next short stretch).

Once in wood see two W.A.s on tree where turn right to follow broad track as it runs parallel with top of wood. Nearly 200 paces on, as track forks, keep to right-hand fork. This continues to hug top of wood for a further 400 yards, where note another waymark on tree left. Now leave your track to fork left, and down a much narrower track for 100 yards or so, to cross stile, exit from wood.

Continue along wide track in line with right edge of field, coming down to climb stile by a gate, and almost at once reach road by P.F. sign.

A brief diversion to the right takes you into Turville village.

Our walk, however, goes left along the road, a quiet leafy lane. Disregard P.F. & B. on left after nearly ¼ mile, but just a little further on past Turville Valley Farm, where lane divides, do go left over stile as sign guides. Walk up meadow to easily seen stile at top ushering you into wood. Then straight up distinct track. Some 60 yards up it inclines left, and rises steeply for further 60 yards to join a congregation of tracks.

Here, go right on **rising** path as W.A. points, i.e. **not** sharp right and down. Our way travels very slowly upwards through the beech hanger, which means on the side of the hill, so if wet beware of slipping. Don't be tempted by any side paths, simply observing a forward course till, after rather more than ½ mile, another gathering of paths is met. Now go left and sharply up as W.A. indicates. Waymarks pinpoint our route as the path twists up to the top of the wood.

At top cross stile into field, and guided by right hedge, go up to far side and over next stile. Beyond it do **not** aim at easily seen stile slightly left, but go forward, with wire fence and tennis court right. A stile will be discovered in right-hand corner of field. Go over it and ahead, soon with wall left, to reach wide gate and emerge on heath.

Now turn right to pass front of Turville Grange, an imposing house built in the early part of the 18th century, and, ignoring drive left, go along rough track. Soon pass a row of brick and flint cottages and reach Turville Heath House. Here go left to join a green way which widens to a clearing and takes you back to road at Turville Heath.

Refreshments. *Bull and Butcher,* Turville.

WALK 3

LANE END
Hanover Hill, Fingest, Mousells Wood.
5 Miles

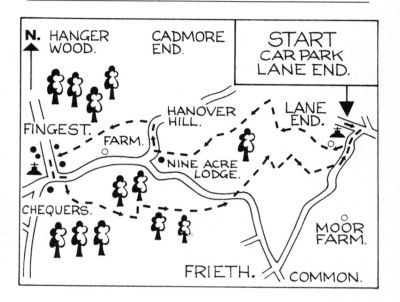

An absolutely superb walk through some of the most beautiful and remote Buckinghamshire country. It would be superfluous to detail them, but there are panoramic views around every other corner. Be prepared for a few ups and downs, plenty of stiles, possibly a little mud here and there at the beginning.

How to get there. By car — to car park in High Street, Lane End.

By bus — Alder Valley 36/37, High Wycombe to Henley. Alight at Lane End.

Leave car park, and go left for a few yards past the post office, then right on road as to Frieth and Hambleden. Soon pass Lane End Church, built in 1878 by J. Oldrid Scott, with roof timbers from a barn of Bisham Abbey, and on reaching a *Jolly Blacksmith* signboard go right on gravel track towards pub. Once there, again go right on P.F. to quickly cross stile. Follow winding path, and as track joins from right, bear left and down to use little bridge over bed of a stream.

Now up, under the beech, as path abides by edge of Finings Wood. When path levels and is joined by another from left, walk on a step or so to take right-hand fork. Larch line the right, but on pastureland appearing left stay ahead, and up, to soon find it bordering either hand. Shortly spy cottage off to right, and go through gateway to common land.

Turn left along the exceptionally broad, rutted track, having an array of golden gorse to right. Just before a metal gate to farm cottage bear left to obvious stile. Over it, bearing right, the way continues with low hedge right to soon develop into a farm track.

When hedge goes round to right, still go forward on distinct path cutting through next field to a stile. Climb, carry on ahead, and on seeing black barn right, walk on down to stile in right-hand corner of field. Beyond, as you follow path downhill, the open slopes of Hanover Hill are to right, whereas on the other hand a fine beech-hanger dips down to the Fingest road.

Another stile is crossed, and you are brought to a road beside Nine Acres Lodge. Seeing Fingest church tower in the distance, walk right along road for about 300 yards where, as road bends right, leave it to maintain your direction along P.F. This means climbing stile to proceed up meadow for 30 yards. Now turn left with hazel hedge, dusty-yellow with catkins in early spring, still to left. Reach stile, cross, and on, slightly uphill. A step or two beyond next stile, **do not go left,** but still ahead. The hedgerow being now to right, the farms in the valley come into view.

When a track joins from right, still go on down to meet a crossing track, where climb stile facing you. Staying on left edge of meadows, walk ahead, over 2 more stiles, to emerge in road at Fingest. Turn left to encounter both the church and the *Chequers.*

The Normans built the church's 60ft. defensive tower, the unusual twin saddleback roof was added some 400 years later. There is only one other like it in the country.

On reaching the *Chequers* our route goes left for 100 yards, where follow P.F. right. It hugs right edge of field, and at far side go on up, wood now right. Glance back at any point here, and you will see why Fingest, viewed from afar, is one of the most photogenic villages in Buckinghamshire.

On achieving the summit, climb stile into Mousells Wood, and follow clear path still uphill. At top of wood go through narrow gap in front of you (W.A. on post) into field. From here it is diagonally left across field's corner, *faint* path, but it is there, taking you back to woodland by means of a wide gap at far side.

A wide track ushers you on along right edge of wood. Ignore various tracks off, but after 250 yards, just prior to seeing a brick wall ahead, turn sharp left directly into wood. About 60 yards on meet a gathering of paths, where go right, and when, in a few more yards, path splits, follow right-hand fork.

Running parallel with the top of the wood, this is a peaceful, sylvan way, where sometimes the only sound is a blackbird scuffling in a bed of dry leaves, the call of a woodpecker or the sudden clatter of a wood pigeon in the tree tops. Stay with it, keeping your direction, despite other paths going hither and thither. Finally reach, and pass, a fenced clearing left, to soon meet wood's boundary.

Here go over stile into meadow. Walk slightly left over grass to kissing-gate in further hedge, and down steps to road. Cross to unmarked gap in opposite hedge, and down to cross stile. Forward up field, to quickly have wood left, as you approach another of the stout stiles which abound around here. Beyond it, continue along right edge of field, wire fence right, till stile spotted right. Climb, then up field path, wire fence now left, for 150 yards. Cross stile on left, and as you walk on, the wire fence is on your right again.

A little short of woodland turn right over stile, and along left edge of field. At next stile go over to follow wire fence, over further stile and on to soon pass through allotments, by some cottages, and emerge on green by road. Turn left, and the path speedily goes past the *Jolly Blacksmith* signboard and back to

Lane End.

Refreshments. *Jolly Blacksmith* and *Chequers* en route, and other pubs in Lane End.

WALK 4

WOOBURN
Berghers Hill, Odds Farm, Dropmore.
5 miles

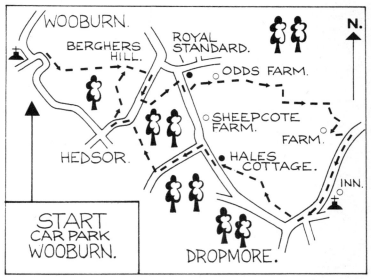

If your idea of a first-class walk is that it should keep turning corners to sustain an element of pleasant surprise, then this excursion does exactly that! It encounters farms, broad fields, hedgerows of thorn, rose, elderberry, hazel, woodlands aglow with rhododendrons in season, a brief stretch of commonland, and is at its most decorative during mid-summer.

How to get there. By car to car park behind Wooburn church.

By bus, Alder Valley No. 20 from High Wycombe to Maidenhead. Alight at Wooburn Church.

The car park faces playing fields, so step out on path travelling up their right boundary, with the houses of Wash Hill on your right. In top right-hand corner go through gap, and instantly turn left up through an undulating field. It is not just a routine right of way, but a generous, inviting path. Once over stile at far side, the path, now bordered by luxuriant hedgerows in which most of our native trees and shrubs seem to have a place, rises slowly.

Towards top, disregard path off right, and go on to soon climb stile. Observe the double signpost here — you'll meet it on returning — and walk forward, rounding The Old Cottage to reach a charming corner of Berghers Hill. Carry on forward along road till you meet further road, and turn right along it for only 130 yards. Then go left on P.F. by the Conifer Nursery; be that as it may, the path takes you into deciduous woodland.

Follow path, ignoring side-tracks, and soon swing left to eventually come to road again by P.F. sign. The *Royal Standard* is seen left, but our way is right along road — there is a footway — for about 150 yards, where take P.F. left. This means crossing over to go up gravel drive towards Odds Farm.

When gravel is replaced by tarmac, use small gate beside cattle grid — not often seen around here — and, unlikely as it seems, walk straight on to pass as improbable a mixture of ancient and modern as one might come upon in many a mile. On one hand is the historic Odds Farm, with the lowest of doors indicating the short stature of our forefathers, and on the other, as you walk on, a neat array of 20th century mobile homes.

At the end, when drive curves, leave it to go ahead over rough stile into field. Having regained completely rural surroundings, proceed along field's left edge, slightly bumpy underfoot but not for long, and at far side cross stile. You may be glad of a helping hand over this one. I wonder if the makers of some stiles ever attempt to cross them! Nevertheless, this one is waymarked to confirm route and once over turn right to have high hedgerow right. The next stile bears the word 'FOOTPATH', and beyond it turn sharp left along edge of adjoining field till you are ushered to another gravel drive. Turn right here. After 200 yards swing right with drive to pass Hicknham Farm, and then bear left on surfaced drive, thus through gateway and down to road by small P.F. sign.

Go right along road, disregard P.F. soon to left, and carry on with woods bounding your left for about ¼ mile to come upon the *Jolly Woodman.*

Situated on the edge of Littleworth Common, the pub, once cottages and stabling belonging to the Dropmore estate, is about a century old, and the little church, passed next, was built at much the same time. Its design, with unusual bargeboards and a bell-turret, is the work of William Butterfield, best known, if not necessarily admired, for Keble College, Oxford.

Immediately beyond church meet road junction, where take no heed of turnings off left, but some 20 yards on do turn right on P.F. through kissing-gate. The narrow path, having run by a garden, then has private woodland right. When stile is met, cross and proceed ahead. Having crossed a farm track, walk forward to enter wood by stile. Path merely edges the beechwood to emerge in road by P.F. sign.

Turn right along road, passing Hales Cottage — footway on opposite side — for 200 yards to turn left as signposted to Burnham. About ¼ mile on, as road bends left, step off it to go right on P. F. & B. Shortly, directly beyond a solitary house, the way develops into a narrower track, briefly entering wood, then journeying outside its left boundary.

This attractive way takes you to road, where a radio mast towers above the distant trees. Walk left along road for no more than 100 yards, then right via gate to follow P. F. & B. going right. At first move parallel with road, but quickly, as path divides, use left fork going slightly downhill amidst the forestry plantation.

Don't be diverted by any branches off, as you go forward till a small 5-bar gate is met. Beyond it, carry on, wood left, pastureland glimpsed through foliage right, to arrive once more at the 2-armed sign behind The Old Cottage.

Turn left to retrace your steps on path which, I'm sure you'll agree, is well worth exploring twice in one outing.

Refreshments. Pubs in Wooburn, and *Royal Standard* along route.

WALK 5

SEER GREEN
Jordans, Butler's Cross, Bowles Farm, Hodgemoor Wood.
4½ miles

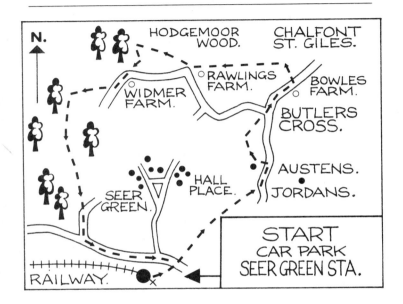

Although this walk touches the fringes of three villages, Seer Green, Jordans and Chalfont St. Giles, it doesn't go through the centre of any of them. Meeting neither pub nor church, nor village shop, the way out is mainly along level fieldpaths and the return through the trees of Hodgemoor Wood and Forestry Commission land. Perhaps at its loveliest in spring and early summer, it is a varied and delightful outing at all times. Allow for some mud if wet.

How to get there. By car — to Station car park.

By train — to Seer Green and Jordans.

By bus — London Country 305 (includes service 455 High Wycombe to Uxbridge).

Leaving the station, car park alongside, walk down the approach to the road, cross and go up Wilton Lane opposite. By-passing all drives off, follow the straight course of this long-used green way. So inviting a lane is it, banked and tree-lined, that it immediately puts one in an appreciative frame of mind.

When finally it becomes surfaced and meets a junction of roads, walk forward past the Wilton Lane sign, to bear left along main road, Twichells Lane. Briefly, we have crossed the invisible boundary into Jordans, and just as speedily, we leave it again. After a few paces, ignore P.F. right, but a further 100 yards on go left on P.F. as if to Harmony Nurseries.

Our path, a drive at first, soon bears left to a house, where leave it to climb stile right into meadow, and on to stile at far side. Beyond, path curves left to next stile below an oak, where four paths congregate. Our route is right on the foot-wide, conspicuous track bisecting the flat fields. It ends at stile ushering you to another meeting of the ways, but this time of the roads at Butlers Cross.

Road walking for a very short spell now, keeping forward as signposted to Chalfont St. Giles. Follow road round for about 200 yards, passing Bowles Farm en route. Then a welcome P.F. sign appears opposite a house called Shearmans, and our way is left along its footpath.

After a few uneven steps climb stile to meadow. The path has petered out, lost beneath a wealth of buttercup, dandelion and the unassuming shepherd's purse. So go diagonally left, and just short of large gap in far corner discover stile. Cross, to proceed by hedge and railings left, over next stile, and on, wire fence now dividing you from distant farm buildings left, to go through inviting gap in far hedgerow.

(The walk is encountering a number of similar meadows, with a scarcity of obvious landmarks. Thus, to avoid going astray, it is as well to remember you should be moving in a westerly direction).

Forward for about 40 yards cutting across corner of meadow, to pass through another gap into adjoining meadow. The path being indistinct, bear right towards middle of right-hand boundary, where come across a stile. Once over, proceed ahead to extreme left-hand corner, i.e. close to stabling. Of the pair of stiles here, use the right-hand one, and without altering your former direction, go on over grazing land to stile in far corner leading by P.F. sign to Rawlings Lane.

Turn right here to enter Hodgemoor Wood, where a Forestry board shows an outline plan of the wood with picnic places, etc. The delightful woodland trails, for both walkers and riders, dispel all notions of Forestry Commission land being solely confined to serried rows of fast-growing conifers.

Our route strolls along the wide bridleway on left. At a fork follow left-hand, still more or less in line with left boundary of wood. In season the woodland floor is carpeted by bluebells. On eventual arrival at an obvious crossing-track, go over towards a HORSE TRAIL notice, but stop short of it to turn left along narrower track marked, appropriately, Forest Walk.

Soon meet a low arch formed by an apple tree, which looks as if it has been lying peacefully on its side for many a long year. (I have found it smothered in blossom).

It is at this stage that our way, going ahead, leaves Hodgemoor Wood to emerge at corner of road. Carry on along level forward road for 250 yards where make a right turn along P.F. & B. Taking an upward, twisting course, the hedged bridlepath mounts to the summit of this little hill. The view opens out just briefly before the path hastens downhill to retreat again beneath the trees. After ¼ mile from the point where you left the road, come down to a collection of paths and signs.

Ignoring stile right, turn sharp left by means of the forest gate to walk through a conifer plantation, and quite quickly emerge at a triangular clearing. There's a double P.F. sign here, and the way is onward, slightly left, via a gap to continue along lower edge of a huge mound of a field.

The next landmark is another forest gate, beyond which carry on along wide track, once more in woodland. When a clearing is met, at a junction of paths, you may spot a half-hidden multiple P.F. sign. But, spot it or not, the way is still forward, with path developing into a broad ride through Blue Close Wood.

When ride ends, and the Forestry land is left behind, proceed ahead by right edge of field. At far side come out to road, Bottom Lane, by P.F. sign. Turn right for 200 yards to road junction. A left turn here will, by following road, deliver you back to station.

Refreshments. Café in Chalfont St. Giles.

Pubs in Seer Green and Chalfont St. Giles.

WALK 6

CHALFONT ST. GILES
Chalfont St. Peter, Three Households, Hill Farm Lane.
5 Miles

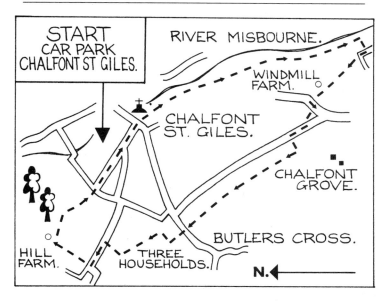

Exploring gentle countryside, yet never far from habitation, this is an amiable walk. The paths, first through the water meadows beside the Misbourne, and returning largely through fields, are unusually level for the Chilterns. The outing may easily be combined with a visit to Milton's cottage at Chalfont St. Giles, though times of opening should be ascertained in advance.

How to get there. By car — to car park behind the library, Chalfont St. Giles.

By bus — London Country 305, High Wycombe to Uxbridge. Alight in village.

As Chalfont St. Giles is one of the few villages of South Buckinghamshire fortunate enough to still have a duck-pond, we will make it the beginning of the walk. So set off up the High Street. Beyond the green, and opposite the Crown, turn left under the fine old lych gate as if to the church.

St. Giles, although Victorian externally, dates back to the 13th century and has some interesting medieval murals and brasses.

Follow the narrow pathway, keeping right of the church grounds till you meet a double stile. Do not go forward, but over stile on right and diagonally over grass to climb another stile. Then turn sharp left and almost immediately over yet another.

The village is left behind as the path leads on between mature thorn bushes. Soon cross further stile, to find the hedges are less high, and orchards, where cattle graze, are seen on either side. After next stile the right hedgerow gives way to sloping meadowland.

From this point our route goes straightforwardly through the meadows, following the course of the Misbourne, which is glimpsed spasmodically.

If, due to hot, dry weather, the Misbourne had dried up, never fear, the paths are well used, and you will have no difficulty. In fact you may notice confirmatory red waymarks on posts and trees, though they mostly point the way you have come.

After four more stiles have been crossed, continue ahead and at far side of meadow a kissing-gate leads on through a copse as you approach Chalfont St. Peter. Beyond next stile you face the grounds of a tennis club. Stay to right of it, thus going behind the pavilion. But about 30 yards beyond it, turn sharp right up an alleyway between houses to reach Boundary Road, Chalfont St. Peter.

As our purpose is to stick to footpaths wherever possible, the route turns directly right again, between the houses to round a corner and cross obvious stile ushering you back to meadowland. Walk slightly left over grass and use kissing-gate to next meadow, identified by a copse of fir and silver birch in far left-hand corner. Follow path slowly up and over another stile marked 'FOOTPATH'.

Now diagonally left to visible wooden gate, and through adjoining kissing-gate. A fenced pathway now takes you on past Windmill Farm to arrive at road.

Turn left along road for 200 yards where go right on P.F. to simply cut off a corner to reach next road. Take no heed of kissing-gate seen directly right, instead go right up road. After a short distance, and just beyond Little Bowstridge, turn left along unmarked track.

Just 50 yards along go right over stile, and then slightly left across meadow to far corner. Here walk on a few steps, copse right, to cross stout stile and forward along track. Once over next stile, go straight on by left edge of meadow to yet another stile. Beyond it, go straight on again. When hedge to your left *turns* left, keep ahead to cross large meadow, passing copse right till you arrive at next stile. Cross, still ahead, hedge now right, to reach stile by a gate. From this point merely continue along attractive hedged lane to emerge in road by a house called Lanners.

This is Three Households, and by going right this road will take you all the way back to St. Giles. But the pleasanter and more rural way is as follows.

Cross road and stile facing you to carry on along right edge of meadow. Go over stile at far side, and the path then turns sharp right by right edge of meadow to its corner. Turn left here, and then simply proceed forward, trees and bushrow right, to cross three more stiles and arrive in more open pasturage. Walk straight over to emerge in Bottrell's Lane by P.F. sign.

Turn left up road till shortly it bends left. Now, ignore conspicuous drive up to brickworks, but leave road by turning right via a kissing-gate and along left edge of field. Beyond stile go on to kissing-gate, and on its other side, house right, find an antiquated signpost. Accept it as a landmark only, though having a long view over the Misbourne valley it is a good place to pause a while.

When ready to move on the way is right along the pretty lane. It is a trifle stony underfoot. This is Hill Farm Lane, which follow all the way down, past intermittent houses including Hunter's Moon, to arrive at road. Cross, and Dodds Lane opposite will deliver you back to Chalfont St. Giles.

WALK 7

PENN
Tylers Green, Penbury Grove Twichels Wood.
3½ miles

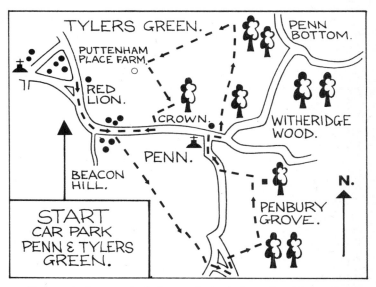

Encountering cool glades and shaded tracks this outing is ideal for a hot and cloudless summer's day. If thirsty, there is a pub about half way round. The route travels along some of the first-class paths roaming south and east of Penn. Although it is mostly level walking Penn is a hill-top village nearly 600ft. above sea level, and there are some grand views.

How to get there. By car — to park near the shops at the merging of Penn and Tylers Green.

By bus — London Country 363, Penn – Totteridge.

Take the *Red Lion* facing the pond as the first landmark, and walk left as signposted to Beaconsfield. Soon pass bus stop and the long flint wall of Rayners School. On spotting Slades Garage right, continue for a further 70 yards to then turn right on P.F. by Little Coppice.

When the hedged way, intially between gardens, crosses drive to Woodlands, keep on as a leafy tunnel takes you into wood. Do not be tempted by stile right, but go ahead to speedily meet a gathering of paths. Turn sharp right and down. This is one of the ancient mule tracks along which men and animals plodded their slow way to the Thames.

Little direction is necessary with so well-defined a track. Merely stroll on beneath the canopy of overhanging branches intertwined with the woody stems of traveller's joy. Rising minimally, the track winds just enough to stimulate a feeling of curiosity as to what is around the next bend.

Eventually it arrives at a small clearing, where still proceed forward as the hedges give way to woodland. Shortly, on spying a 5-bar gate ahead, look out for and turn along path branching off right. It delivers you quickly to road by P.F. & B. sign. Cross, turn left to go along the farther of the two roads, thus moving downhill. As road bends right take no heed of P.F. right, but walk on down beech-lined road for 100 yards to meet further road junction. Turn very sharp left, thus making a 'V' turn, along the lower road.

After 150 yards, go right, being guided by a 2-armed sign over stile to climb gradually uphill. Again there is a casual archway of foliage, and when, at the top, you emerge from it, manipulate the stile before you. Now turn left on drive/lane, orchards of Underwood right, and on the other hand a widespread vista across fields with more, or less, of Penn church seen according to the state of the greenery!

Presently, the playing fields of Penbury Grove, a school for deaf children, appear right. Once beyond school house and buildings go left. There's a W.A. on a post to guide you, but the path is very clear as it follows left edge of field to stile which takes you to road. By going right up road, (Paul's Hill) you will reach the historic church and Penn's tiny village green.

In past days this was the village centre, church, pub, and stocks on the green all in the customary tight-knit group.

Cross road to gain both the *Crown* and the superlative view over Penn Bottom. Turn right and immediately beyond the pub's car park turn left along P.F. It skirts the grounds of the *Crown,* encounters a pair of stiles, looking stout enough to withstand all eventualities, and enters Vicarage Wood. Follow path in line with right boundary as W.A. guides. When finally it splits, take left fork journeying down and out of wood by stile into field.

From here a brick farmhouse, enviably situated in a sequestered corner, is the only sign of habitation. But a well trodden flinty track beckons the walker on straight across the field, and swiftly down into the valley. Climb stile before you and instantly go left alongside hedge left till far boundary is reached. Over next stile, and on, hedge still left, though imperceptibly the direction has veered slightly left, away from the outbuildings of the 500-year-old Puttenham Place, Penn's oldest farm.

On coming to wood left, carry on for a few paces to cross stile on left, and into Twichels Wood, for a brief diversion.

Rooks nest in the tops of many of the typically straight beech, and like other birds nesting in colonies, noisily draw attention to their chosen habitat.

Our path winds up below the beech, and suddenly decides to abandon the wood and regain the field by means of a stile. Go half left up bumpy grassland, and in far corner a couple of adjacent stiles lead you back up to road. By turning right and through Penn village it is but ½ mile to the *Red Lion.*

Refreshments. *Red Lion* and *Crown* in Penn.

WALK 8

BRADENHAM
Bradenham Village, Smalldean Farm, Park Wood.
3 Miles

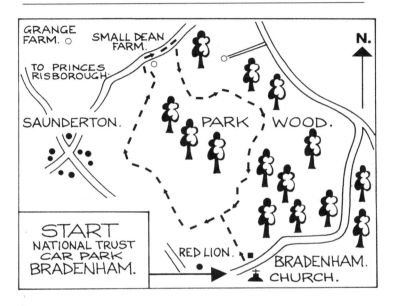

Short enough to tempt even the most inexperienced of ramblers, Bradenham, once the home of Disraeli's family, has probably altered less over the last hundred years than any other village in South Buckinghamshire. Even before it passed into the guardianship of the National Trust, the last manorial owner had worked hard to preserve the *status quo*. Visually, the village, dotted at spacious intervals around the broad green, is much as it was in feudal times. The bordering countryside is equally unspoilt.

How to get there. By car — to National Trust car park, Bradenham.

31

The church of St. Botolphs, looking down the green, is a suitable point from which to begin.

Leaving the church, walk to the road, cross, and a yard or so to the right take P.F. setting off past the Youth Hostel — a small brick and flint building where previously the village children were schooled. Almost at once climb two stiles in rapid succession to continue along path curving purposefully on between farmland. On meeting a crossing track at end of field, move couple of steps left, to then resume your former direction.

The ample grass track rises gradually, and on the right lush grass is masking the remains of a hedge. A backward glance is called for here to see peaceful Bradenham against its background of woods.

Nearing the top, go over stile by gate, cross a rutted track emerging from wood, over further stile and forward, wood now right.

Should you come this way in spring be on the lookout for scatterings of primroses and violets from now onwards.

The houses of Saunderton appear away to left, and when you reach far corner of this field bear round and down as waymark on 5-bar gate shows. Walk down the springy turf, and at bottom of field go through gap. Steeply downhill for a few paces, and ahead for about 50 yards to find a green footpath sign at a corner. Turn right along a further inviting fieldpath, wood still right. The generous, unrestricting width of all these paths makes one feel welcome.

After only a further 50 yards again go right, as sign directs. Thus farmland stretches out to left, and a hedgerow composed of varied woodland trees adds interest to your other side. In autumn it is aglow with the bright berries of the Wayfaring Tree. Like the wild clematis, traveller's joy, it is a plant so named because of its frequency beside the original tracks which our ancestors of long ago trod out over the chalk hills.

Stay with path as farm outbuildings are seen ahead. On eventual arrival at end of field, climb stile and turn sharp left down edge of meadow to next visible stile. Beyond it bear right on clear path winding between the barns of Smalldean Farm to emerge in road by P.F. sign.

Turn right along road, no more than a lane in fact, for 250 yards where, rather surprisingly, see a small car park by a

National Trust board. Here, a sign directs you right up to and through a wide waymarked gate. Continue up the well-banked track leading into Park Wood.

Be careful to avoid all diversions off, some of which are indicated by red arrows, and stick to the main pedestrian track, waymarked by a series of white arrows. Soon veering vaguely left, it rises fairly sharply, and at a distinct split follow forward left fork, still uphill. Again at a further division, take the left-hand fork, quickly confirmed by W.A.

Winding a little now, houses are shortly glimpsed through the trees. Also see a wire fence dividing wood from a clearing planted with beech saplings. Here bear right and with fence on your left follow it till it makes a right-angled turn to the left. At this point go right for a few steps only, then left as distinct waymark guides.

The track now takes a downward trend hurrying to reach the valley floor. At the bottom walk immediately right, away from signs of civilisation, and stroll on down the beechwood track. Beech finally give way to the universal conifer. In fact conifers in varying stages of maturity greet the eye in their customary serried rows.

Where, on approaching a larch plantation, the track splits, take right fork. Keep ahead till you pass a group of tall pines right. Now turn right with track going up briefly to reach a fine broad ride. Go left along it with Bradenham church and Manor, the 17th-century mansion which was once the home of Isaac d'Israeli, father of 'Dizzy', forming a tranquil picture ahead.

At bottom of ride go right over stile by gate, and along fieldpath, low hedge left. Hedge ends at a gap and the crossing track met at beginning of walk. Simply turn left to retrace your steps to the village.

Refreshments. The *Red Lion,* Bradenham.

WALK 9

AMERSHAM — OLD TOWN
The Market Hall, Mop End, Shardeloes Park.
5 or 3½ Miles

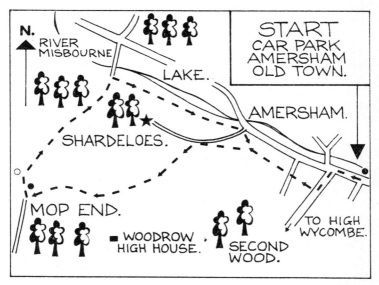

Amersham has long been a centre for ramblers. And if these all-seasons footpaths are more frequented than some, they are no less enjoyable for being popular. You *may* see a variety of waterfowl on Shardeloes lake; though both the Misbourne, which was dammed to form this ornamental water, and the lake can be dry at times. The unpredictability is of interest in itself! It's been a local talking point for years!

How to get there. By car — to car park in the The Broadway, Amersham — Old Town. (For shorter walk: use lay-by on the A413 at entrance to Shardeloes and pick up walk at [A]).

By bus — Various buses and green line coaches, alight at bus station.

34

Take the bus station, a few yards from the car park, as the first landmark. Set off towards the Market Hall, and once past the Memorial Gardens turn left up Whielden Street. Shortly after passing Sundial Antiques, look out for, and turn right, up a marked P.F. between houses. It leads you through The Platt — an obsolete name for a plot of ground, in this case probably for tenants of the manor of Shardeloes — and on to pass the endearing, much photographed Chimney Cottage right.

Follow the wide path ahead, narrowing to skirt small cemetery left. A stranger to the town might well be unaware of this twisting path, a direct link between village and Shardeloes, hidden away behind the High Street. So, having discovered it, continue forward to go through two successive kissing-gates and reach a road, Cherry Lane. Cross, and pass through opposite gate to walk on with field sloping up to left, and sounds from a nearby rookery.

When you arrive at a P.F. sign, where right-hand hedge ceases, take left fork up and across the expanse of field, once known as One Tree Field, with Shardeloes soon hoving into view. At far side emerge, via kissing-gate, by a P.F. sign. A step or so left see a similar gate.

[A] If on short route, walk from lay-by up drive to reach this gate, which bears a sign 'To Mop End 1½ miles'. As that is where we are going, the walk continues through gate, where path goes unmistakably along the floor of the valley, soon to have fir plantation left. This is then replaced by hedge, and when it ends and a fence faces you, go right for a pace or two to cross stile. From here path bears right round wood right, and passes the Mop End power station. Disregarding all tracks off, keep to broad path till station is passed, and you reach a pylon right. Then veer right to enter woodland; the way is quite clear.

Walk along woodland track, initially well shaded, then opening out till it comes to road. Turn right for 60 yards, passing Rose Cottage, to arrive at Mop End Farm. Again go right on P.F. & B., an ancient cart track known as Mop End Lane. For approximately the first mile hedgerows protect both sides.

The circuitous route up to Mop End almost disguises the fact that it is uphill all the way, but now it is plain that the lane is making a slow descent.

When the left hedgerow gives way to a plantation of fir, the view opens up briefly. After that, still on its downward trek, the way is lightly shaded as it brings you down to the parkland of Shardeloes. You will see a kissing-gate on right which pass through; it bears the helpful words 'Footpath to Amersham'.

The much favoured path goes steadily through the park. When it eventually bends right, leave it to walk forward over grass for about 100 yards to stile. There are, in fact, a pair to be climbed, and then still ahead, slightly left as path moves to edge the lake.

Now there is an unobstructed view of the 18th-century mansion on the crest of the hill. Originally built by Stiff Leadbetter for William Drake, the manorial owner, it was completed by Robert Adam, and is believed to be his earliest work. It is now converted into flats.

Even if the lake is not full, keep a watch for bird life amidst the reeds. When stile is met, cross and go on. As lake ends walk ahead to go through kissing-gate. Then over meadow to stile ushering you to the cricket ground. Turn left, walk behind pavilion and reach Shardeloes drive by a P.F. sign.

From here, turn left to road and by going right you will return to Amersham. Alternatively, to avoid road, from the P.F. sign cross drive to use kissing-gate opposite. Follow clear green path cutting across corner of field to arrive at a P.F. sign by corner of hedge, which you will recognise, and you now have only to retrace your steps to the starting point.

Refreshments. Cafés in High Street, Amersham; wide choice of pubs.

WALK 10

LITTLE MISSENDEN
Little Kingshill, Boot Farm, Holmer Green.
4 Miles

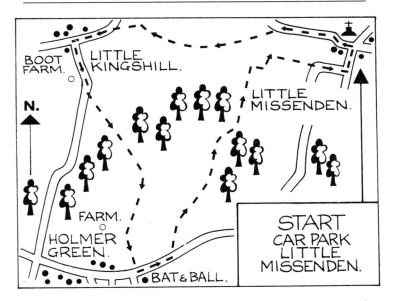

Little Missenden, with its one thousand-year-old church is one of Buckinghamshire's most attractive villages. This short but really lovely walk explores the village, and some of the lanes and meadowland to the south and west.

How to get there. By car to park in village. Alternative parking is possible at Holmer Green, in which case pick up walk from [A]

From Little Missenden church set off westwards, i.e. with church wall on right.

The Church of St. John Baptist dates back to Anglo-Saxon days, and is renowned for its medieval wall paintings. Full details of its very interesting history are to be found inside.

As wall ends see P.F. but ignore and continue along road till houses on left cease, where cross stile by P.F. sign. Walk diagonally over meadow in line with telegraph poles. At far side cross two stiles and the intervening lane, to maintain your direction over meadowland which slopes down to left, and still in line with poles.

Climb next stile, then ahead along distinct path cutting straight across an extensive field. When it ends carry on along lane for some 150 yards to road. Turn left to pass a 'Little Kingshill' board, and follow road — there is a footway.

After about 350 yards turn left as signposted to Holmer Green. A further 350 yards, having passed picturesque Boot Farm right, turn left down a driveway. Just a few steps down see a P.F. & B. sign, at which bear right, thus leaving driveway to take the narrower, unsurfaced path.

Rooks inhabit the tree tops here, far from any earthbound enemies. Even out of the nesting season they frequently visit their chosen trees.

To continue, stay with this shaded way, moving downhill. Soon it rises again, you may then observe a stile left and paths entering wood right. **Use as landmarks only,** and keep ahead to arrive at a broad crossing lane. Take no heed of stile facing you, but turn right along the lane, which, after just over ¼ mile, becomes surfaced and brings you to a 'Featherbed Lane' sign and the road at Holmer Green.

[A] The *Bat and Ball* can be spotted to right, though our route goes left along the road (it is Penfold Lane linking Holmer Green and Little Missenden). Disregard P.F. left after about 150 yards, but do go left on the next one, more accurately a bridleway, a further 100 yards on.

Once past farm buildings left — there could be farm mud around — and a pleasing house right, the path emerges as a more open track. A good track to amble along, casting an eye over the low hedges to the farmland beyond; hedges where the yellow-hammer may well be hopping along before you ('hedge-hopper' is its country name).

On arrival at a definite fork, keep to forward right path entering woodland. Again at next fork, abide by the right-hand, thus going on through wood till towards its far boundary the houses of Little Missenden are glimpsed through the trees.

Soon path curves and begins to level out. When it suddenly broadens and double gates appear on either side, go right over stile and along green path making its well defined course across the field. This brings you back to road, Penfold Lane again, where by turning left you will shortly regain the village of Little Missenden.

Refreshments. Pubs in Little Missenden and Holmer Green.

WALK 11

GREAT MISSENDEN
Rignall Farm, Prestwood, Angling Spring Wood.
4 Miles

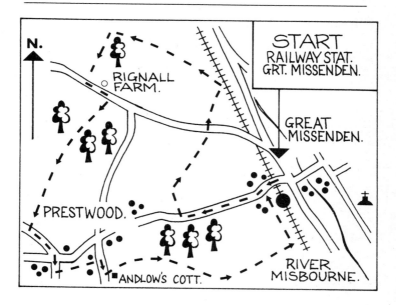

After a short stretch of road, climbing up out of the Misbourne valley, this route explores some of the inviting beechwood tracks and meadow paths to the west of Great Missenden. Bluebells add to its charm in May.

How to get there. By car — to car park in road beside Great Missenden library.

By train — to Great Missenden.

By bus — Alder Valley 27/27a High Wycombe to Great Missenden. London Country 359 Amersham to Lee Common (no Sunday service).

Station, bus stop and car park being conveniently grouped together, let's begin from the station. Cross the bridge over railway, and go on up Martinsend Lane. Quite a stiff climb, but continue up, by-passing all footpaths and turnings off, till you arrive at a 2-armed P.F. sign on left. Here go right along Upper Hollis which is on the opposite side of the road from the footway. Continue along until Upper Hollis bends distinctly left, where leave it to walk forward on P.F.

As it takes you to pass a bungalow left, and a row of larch right, the houses are left behind and the prospect opens out.

Keep to path as larch is replaced by hedgerow, and now there is a glimpse of the roof of the *Black Horse* on the far side of the railway. It is a focal point, because from the meadow facing it, unseen from this distance, springs the source of the River Misbourne.

On coming down to road (Rignall Road) by P.F. sign, cross, walk about 20 yards left to follow P.F. through gate into meadow. Not well defined here, the path curves right, and once past houses right, aim at visible tunnel under railway. However, just short of it turn left towards hedge at far side of meadow. Of the two easily spotted stiles, cross the one on right, to reach an arable field.

Follow single file, well-trodden path up field. At top go up steep bank which, if it has rained, it is easier to slip down than walk up. Then path turns left to negotiate corner of next field, and continues along its edge till you are faced by woodland. Here leave field to bear left and enter Coneybank Wood. A leaf-strewn track guides you through the wood, and on coming out at far side turn left down broad way.

On meeting surfaced road, carry on down under an avenue of chestnuts. At end by P.F. sign, and 'Mapridge Green Lane' sign, turn left along verge, passing Rignall Farm, for about 120 yards. Take right turn here as sign guides. The first few steps are up a driveway, but once past house go forward with fence left, hedge right, to quickly climb stile to meadow.

Walk up meadow beside hedge, largely hazel. At top, a stile leads into Rignall Wood. Keep to footpath, moving steadily up between the trees to eventually arrive in open ground. Veer slightly left on farm track bounding left edge of extensive field.

Shortly, a sign directs you onwards, but to right of

hedgerow. After crossing three more stiles, a concrete drive leads to road, Moat Lane, in Prestwood.

Turn left along Moat Lane to reach the High Street. Cross, and on by way of Nairdwood Lane for 100 yards where turn left along alleyway, marked 'No Cycling'. At far end cross road and walk down short length of New Road, and then along P.F. before you. It takes you first past Andlows Cottage, right, and then edges farmland as it travels down to Angling Spring Wood.

Once in wood ignore all side paths, and simply walk on the delightful track straight down valley of wood to its further boundary where stands a 3-armed signpost. Use stile facing you to continue on broad field track. The grey tower of Great Missenden Church is seen ahead above the town. Track delivers you to road beside the railway. Turn left along it to return to Martinsend Lane and the station.

Refreshments. The Coffee House — Great Missenden. Pubs in Great Missenden and Prestwood.

WALK 12

GREAT HAMPDEN
Hampden Row, Hampden House, Redland End.
3 Miles.

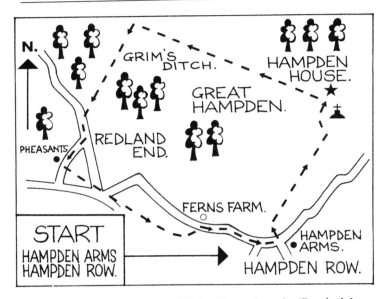

Hampden was the home of John Hampden, the 'Patriot', but the Hampden estate, excellent walking country, has even earlier association of interest for it is crossed by one of the county's best preserved and most readily identified sections of the prehistoric Grim's Ditch.

This is a level route, along which every stretch of the path seems to have an individual charm of its own.

How to get there. By car to Hampden Row.

Parking is possible beside the common near the *Hampden Arms*, from which point the walk sets off.

Walk from the pub the few steps to the road junction,

43

marked by signpost, and go right on the 'Private, No Through Road'. It swings right to bring you to P.F. which follow to pass low barn right, and a thatched cottage, half hidden by shrubs, left. Soon pass a stile, and continue on green path. When larch trees on the left cease, go through gap to find fields all about you.

Keep forward, cross a tarmac drive and climb stile to come upon an engaging and truly pastoral scene. Sheep dot the parkland, or huddle under the trees; and before you, shielded by its protective foliage, is the grey church. It is eternally identified with John Hampden, whose name has become synonymous with the independent spirit of the people of Buckinghamshire.

The major part of Hampden's life was spent here — we shall see his home, Hampden House, in a step or so. His father was a wealthy Buckinghamshire squire, and he was, on his mother's side, a first cousin of Oliver Cromwell. He rode out one January morning to make his unprecendented stand against the Monarchy and payment of the ship-money levy. A few years later he gave his life for the Parliamentarian cause and was buried here at Great Hampden.

Our walk goes straight on to enter the church grounds by way of a kissing-gate. A clear path leads you round the church and out to a drive facing Hampden House, now a school and much altered since Hampden's day.

Go left along drive. Once past the converted stable block a white gate before you leads on along a broad green track, and, looking over your shoulder, you have a good view of the front of the house and the magnificent cedars. When a gate is met, go through and walk up to path which follow along right edge of field. Ignore paths off, and keep on as the very inviting track runs parallel with the distinctive line of beech edging the earthworks of Grim's Ditch.

When conifer saplings spring up left, go through gate and ahead. But on arrival at far corner of field, where all paths just ask to be explored, steer away from stile under a Spanish chestnut, to walk left. Thus a mixed plantation now screens your right hand. It ends at a stile, beyond which a shadowed path winds through the beechwood.

On meeting a crossing track bear right with it for a yard or two, as a tree-felling area is seen ahead. Skirt this clearing by bearing left and following path along bank, then between beech to reach stile and road at Redland End. Turn left, and very shortly right down road as to Loosley Row. After 150 yards, just past a house called Pheasants, go **left** over stile as indicated by double P.F. sign across the road. A path takes you over an enchanting patch of grassland where tall ox-eyed daisies grow.

At far side arrive at road. Cross, walk over apron of green on which stands a signpost, and again cross a road to follow P.F. over high stile, meant for giants I think!

A conspicuous path wends its way through the beechwoods of the Hampden estate. Inclining slightly right, with an occasional waymark to encourage you, the way is easily observed. On coming to a distinct crossing track, still proceed ahead as W.A. shows, open to the sky now, with a variety of trees to either side. Pass a small clearing right, and as track joins from right, bear left to almost at once reach road opposite Ferns Farm.

By turning right you will regain the *Hampden Arms.*

Refreshments. *Hampden Arms,* and Hampden Common on which to picnic.

WALK 13

GREAT KIMBLE
Happy Valley, Chequers and Ridgeway, Buckmoorend.
3½ Miles

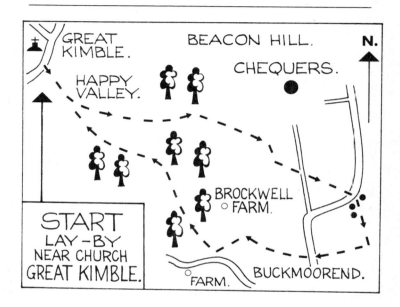

Needless to say, the aim of these walks is to tread the footpath way, and to avoid the roads wherever possible. This one touches the tarmac only where it crosses a minor road near Chequers. Moreover, it wanders through some of the really splendid wooded and hilly country around the Chequers estate, including the B.B.O.N.T. Nature Reserve above Happy Valley. Though short enough to be covered in an hour at a steady pace, there are such a multitude of glorious spots at which to linger that I do suggest allowing a longer time — plus picnic perhaps. We call the Chilterns gentle hills, yet the views from some of the escarpments, as here, hold a touch of drama.

How to get there. By car to lay-by just south of Great Kimble church.

From the lay-by, where stands the picture-book Cymbeline's Cottage, walk up the obvious P.F. & B. Rising steadily, the centuries-old way has bushrows linked by the entwining growth of the wild clematis, or traveller's joy. After ¼ mile find a kissing-gate on left acting as entrance to the Nature Reserve. Owned by the very active Bucks, Berks and Oxon Naturalist Trust, it is one of their latest acquisitions.

Once through gate, follow the clear path diagonally up the parkland of the Reserve, with the deep coombe of Happy Valley, or Great Kimble Warren, away to left. Glancing back there is one of the fine views to the plain of Aylesbury, which are such a feature of this escarpment. Soon the path passes below one or two low spreading beech. When the wire fencing enclosing Happy Valley is reached, bear left beside it.

Shortly see stile left of your path, ignore and go on to find two more at top of rise. Use the right-hand one to leave the Reserve, and follow path bisecting arable field. At far side note a Ridgeway post, where veer right to a second one by stile, which cross.

There is no mistaking the path as you walk on with Chequers Court seen emerging from the distant trees off to your left, and the Coombe Hill Monument, stark against the sky, acting as a further landmark. Having passed a clearing in the woodland to your right, the beech takes over again, and on arrival at stile, climb and stay with path which has taken a right turn. After 60 yards turn left over another stile.

This is the re-routed Chequers path about which there was such a to-do. Apart from the significant fact that, briefly, the house disappears from view, the walker has little cause for complaint. He still has a green and rural path to tread, and the deviation is minimal.

Walk on down the field to then go ahead over 3 stiles, one after the other, and thus reach further parkland on far side of Victory Drive. Now the way leads on quite distinctly, rounds a clump of beech, and goes over an unusual set of metal steps — correctly also a stile, because it ushers us on, and is a bar to livestock — to arrive in road at Buckmoorend.

47

We have been keeping pace with the Ridgeway for some while, but here we part company. So cross road and walk up surfaced drive to pass whitewashed cottages left; the plaque they bear, L. of F. 1920, refers, of course, to Lord Lee of Fareham, who gave Chequers to the nation.

Within a few steps or so, pass some barns right, distinguished by a clock-face — it works too! Immediately beyond the last house, as drive becomes a winding lane, abandon it by turning right (i.e. beside garden) on single file path. Unmarked, it is more clearly seen where it forges ahead through the field, and when you reach far extremity of field and emerge on road there is a P.F. sign to confirm the path. Cross, with care as always, walk a step or so left, then go right on P.F. Within yards pass through gateway, briefly beside field, before path delves into the beechwood.

Stay with path meandering close to wood's right boundary, with intermittent glimpses of Chequers and Coombe Hill. On arrival at a pair of stout white gateposts, go between them and forward. There is a clearing to be walked through, and beyond it meet a broad crossing track. Turn right along it to again move in line with right boundary of a wood (Pulpit wood), until narrowing, path goes further in once more. You are not likely to mistake the way if you just follow the track till suddenly it comes out into the open and gives a view of Beacon Hill crowned by its lonely group of beech; Happy Valley, with its wonderful array of variegated greens; and, below the hills, the grey-blue plain.

Shortly the path begins to descend more noticeably, and on seeing a waymarked stile right, disregard this and all other diversions to either side as you carry on down. Should it have rained recently it can be slippery.

The Nature Reserve re-appears right, and very soon you will arrive at the kissing-gate you'll recognise. From here simply walk on downhill the way you came up to regain Great Kimble.

Refreshments. *Bernard Arms,* Great Kimble.

WALK 14

WENDOVER
Bacombe Hill, Coombe Hill, Dunsmore.
4 Miles

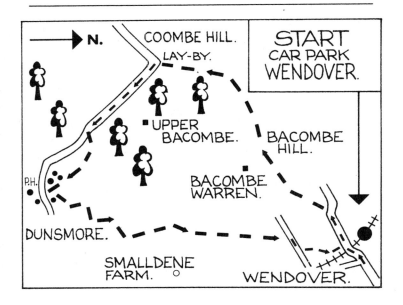

Good firm paths ensure this is an all-the-year-round walk. Going up Coombe Hill, which at 852ft. above sea level is accepted as one of the highest points in the Chilterns, is an exhilarating outing. One of the enchantments is the panoramic views, so if you have binoculars don't forget to take them. View-finding apart, this route wanders over glorious country. In choosing your starting-point (see below) it may be helpful to remember that from the alternative car park the climb up Coombe Hill is at the end of the walk, instead of the beginning.

How to get there. By car — to car park in Wendover High Street.

OR — to lay-by where the Dunsmore road bends and reaches a gateway to Coombe Hill, 1 mile N.W. of Dunsmore, and start walk at [A]

By train — to Wendover.

From Wendover High Street walk up over the railway bridge, station seen to right. Ignore P.F. left, and another soon to right, as you continue up the Ellesborough Road, which follows the route of the Icknield Way. About 300 yards from bridge, where road bends right, leave it — crossing with caution as cars can whizz round that bend — to take P.F. left. With a choice of two tracks going up Bacombe Hill, use the right-hand one, signed 'No Horses'. You will see a white acorn denoting it as part of the Ridgeway path.

When it splits use left fork, and keep forward, dis-regarding paths to either side. (As long as you go on and up, do not worry too much about which path — they are numerous — and we are aiming at the top and the Monument). Shortly, steps appear ahead, and by using them you will gain your first viewpoint, and, if weary, a seat!

This path soon merges with a lower parallel path, and expands into a broad ride. From here, onwards to the summit of Coombe Hill, there are panoramic views over the Vale of Aylesbury and beyond to Oxfordshire.

When wooden fencing stretches out over turf, use stile in middle and go on. Temporarily the way changes in character, becoming a pathway shadowed by shrubs and trees. On opening out again, still go onwards — the rise is very gradual — till a wooden kissing-gate is met. Once through, continue on over the close-cropped turf to reach the Monument seen ahead.

The Coombe Hill Monument was built in memory of men who fell in the Boer War. It is an outstanding landmark for miles around, and from this superb hill-top one can look across the wonderful undulating country.

Having relaxed and absorbed the view, carry on by turning sharp left away from the Monument, thus walking between two wooden seats. The path is not so clearly defined at this point, but by bearing left you will quickly strike a path moving south-east towards wood seen off to left.

Beside wood discover an unmistakable, partly cobbled track

along which keep forward, close to boundary of wood. It brings you past a National Trust signboard, and through swing gate to corner of the Dunsmore road and a parking area.

[A] From swing gate walk forward along road, which has a splendid breadth of verge below a clipped hedge on right, while on the other side branches of thorn, crabapple, beech, hornbeam, oak, all of remarkably uniform height, bow gracefully towards the road.

About ¼ mile on, ignore P.F. left and go on to pass three highly individual houses within yards of each other. Again ignore P.F. left, and 70 yards further on note P.F. sign right as **landmark only,** as you go **left** straight up into wood.

The track is perfectly clear, and disregarding several off-shoots to left, walk on shortly to be travelling east then south-east. When the track, though still in wood, is confined by wire fencing, keep on to come out by house and a P.F. sign.

This is the hamlet of Dunsmore, and by making a short diversion right you will reach the *Fox,* — the duck-pond at the cross-roads, and the *Black Horse.*

Our route however is left, following line of metal fencing till it ceases. Don't be tempted here by the woodland track off left, but carry on ahead with meadows, now on both sides, encircled by trees. The silvery foliage of whitebeam catches the eye, the yellowish-green of oak, and the more sombre hues of the taller firs.

As the meadows end, the path retreats beneath the trees' shade, going down steadily till it sallies forth into the open again, with a prospect over the valley to Wendover Woods. Two paths face you. Follow the left, descending fairly steeply beside the left-hand wood. Just 200 yards on, the way is again lined by metal railings as it re-enters wood.

When path swings left and sharply up, go with it. On it levelling, then slowly descending, there are enticing vistas through the foliage right. At a further swing left, disregard stile off to right, and follow your path which also leads down to a stile.

The prospect changes — the scenic variety is one of the joys of this walk. Woodland is left behind, and a chalk path leads you on through a field. Towards the distant horizon, Halton House, one-time home of Alfred de Rothschild, stands out above the rolling farmland.

On approaching next stile, much of the view is temporarily eclipsed by a steep bank. Over stile bear left straight up the daisy-scattered bank, which with its low bushes of briar and thorn is a delightfully undisturbed corner of the countryside.

It is worth looking back, to see the wide curve of chalk you've just trodden; the chalk which has formed the landscape of the Chilterns.

Go over next stile to find path crossing another field, and then, with gardens on either side, emerging in a minor road, Bacombe Warren. Turn right for 130 yards only, and left via stile to follow yet a further well-defined chalk footway through fields. One more stile to be clambered over, and the way returns you directly to Ellesborough Road, where turn right for Wendover.

Refreshments. Pubs in Dunsmore and Wendover. Café in Wendover.

WALK 15

WADDESDON
Waddesdon Manor, Windmill Hill Farm, Westcott.
4 Miles

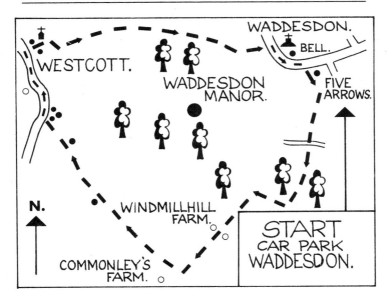

Waddesdon Manor, the fabulous Rothschild mansion now owned by the National Trust, crowns a hill at the edge of the village. The countryside at its foot, encompassed by mainly level paths, has its own natural beauty, and the Manor itself is a central landmark glimpsed intermittently. Enhanced by the splendour of the Waddesdon trees it is a lovely walk at all times.

How to get there. By car — to Waddesdon and park in the village, or in a lay-by off the A41 nearby.

By bus — Red Rover 1, 15, 16, Aylesbury-Waddesdon. Alight in village. No Sunday service.

Beside the *Five Arrows,* some 60 yards short of the entrance to the Manor, stands the War Memorial. Set off down the private road running behind it, ignoring P.F. seen to right within first few steps. Very speedily you will pass the estate office right, and walk between tall brick piers to enter the wooded Waddesdon estate. Carry on, and when path comes out to open parkland follow right fork, thus bowling green is passed right.

Shortly arrive at, and disregard, a crossing track, and continue ahead. A clump of fine chestnuts will be seen left. About here the roof and decorative chimneys of the Manor itself appear away to right.

Keep to path as it curves towards Windmill Hill Farm, going gently uphill now. From this angle Waddesdon, just topping the trees, resembles a fairy-tale castle. It was, in fact, designed in Chateau style by Gabriel Hippolytte Destailleur for Baron Ferdinand de Rothschild. In 1874, with a masterly eye for a good site, Rothschild bought up the hill and adjoining land. During the following years a transformation took place. First the top of the hill was sliced off, and then a special steam railway and teams of horses from France were employed to transport materials to the site. As the house rose from its foundations its spectacular extravagance must surely have amazed the village.

Bending left as it levels, the path is briefly shaded by trees, and beyond them a wide track journeys right. However, tempting as it appears, disregard and keep forward. A concrete drive leads you to enter a farmyard through a green metal gate.

The rest of the walk is mostly through farmland, so please do be exceptionally diligent in closing all gates behind you, making certain they are secured.

Once in farmyard, house left, walk straight ahead with barns on either hand, to meet a tall Dutch barn. Here, still on concrete, bear left then right to red metal gate and, leaving farm behind, go on down path. The row of elms to the left ends at a red brick cottage, and past it a further gate brings you to the top of a field. More elms appear left, so walk down beside them, and at the bottom where there are two red gates, use the one facing you, not to the right. Once through then turn right along broad, well-kept bridleway — not marked as such.

Agricultural land sweeps out to the horizon. Elms, the

typical English wayside tree, still act as boundaries, but, alas, as everywhere the destructive beetle is taking its toll. At field's far side a further gate ushers you on over next field. As yet another field is entered, hedgerow right, just continue forward. Once past its far boundary pass a semi-derelict brick barn, and proceed ahead, as gravel drive develops on approach to new agricultural buildings. Concrete replaces gravel, and the way passes the buildings and some houses to reach road.

Turn right towards Westcott along the Ashendon Road although there are no signs to indicate it's name at this point. Having passed both Linnet Drive and Raven Crescent right, and Wescott Farm on the other side, look out for, and turn right along Lower Green. Pass the tiny Catholic church, and when road bends left abandon it to go right on P.F.

Climb two stiles, and go ahead over grass — there is a pair of intriguing cottages with deep overhanging thatch seen right. Take heed here, and when barbed wire left ceases go a couple of large paces left, to climb fence/stile on your right. Path is hardly perceptible, but bear half-left over grass and over stile at far side, which is really a pair bridging a ditch, and then the path cuts clearly through arable land and proceeds to be bounded right by wire and post fence. Reach a small stile where a cinder track leads you on, soon to become a tarmac way sheltered by a long brick wall, with greenhouse left.

When wall ends ignore side tracks and carry on to emerge on road with Waddesdon church seen ahead. Nearly back now, of course, but don't miss catching a glimpse of the thatched well, clearly visible from road at entrance to the yard of the many-gabled stables passed on left.

On arrival at road turn right past the *Bell* for 150 yards to regain the War Memorial.

Refreshments. Inns in village and tea-room at Waddesdon Manor when open. (Fee payable to enter National Trust grounds).

WALK 16

QUAINTON
Hill End Farm, Quainton Hill.
4 Miles

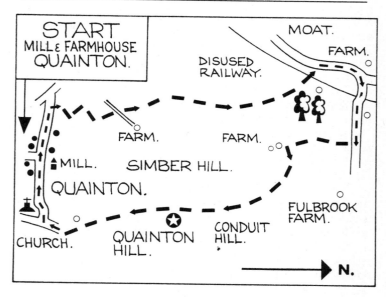

A truly rural and varied all-the-year-round walk. Near Quainton a series of little hills belie the usually accepted belief that the county north of Aylesbury is wholly flat. Be prepared then for the one or two short climbs from which are gained panoramic views, and an easy trot down again! Moreover, the route explores the most interesting parts of this absolutely delightful village, the birthplace of George Lipscomb, the county's own historian.

How to get there. By car to park by The Green.

The top of The Green harbours the remains of a medieval village cross. Behind it is the substantial 18th-century Cross

Farmhouse, and even higher up is the sail-less structure of a tower mill, some 100ft. tall. With your back to the farmhouse and mill, turn right along Upper Street. Ignore inviting P.F. after about 200 yards, but when road starts to dip go right on tarmac P.F. between houses. After a step or so move left onto narrow path quickly becoming hedged. Go through gate and proceed ahead, to soon bear sharp left and down.

When cobbles underfoot cease turn right, thus gardens are left, and when elms to right end, climb stile into meadow. Signs of the path have vanished, but make your way slightly left in direction of white gate in far left-hand corner. Here cross stile left and go through the white gate but **not** ahead on gravel drive. Instead, bear half-left over grass, to soon have hedge left, and keep in line with it to far corner of field.

Now the route continues forward by means of stile/fence facing you, and along left edge of next field. On arriving at far corner cross double stile bridging ditch, and carry on beside lofty hedgerow, mainly bramble. When further boundary is met, ignore gate left, and walk ahead negotiating gate to arrive in yet another meadow. Don't change direction, but go across grass to gate in far hedge, slightly left, with an isolated farm seen tucked into the lee of the hill away right. Go through gate and on along grass path — fairly clearly defined here.

There is a further gate, and the way then proceeds till you arrive at a lone willow clump. At this point bear right as narrow path takes you on and out of meadowland by some metal rails. Walk left through the waste land to emerge in road by P.F. sign. Turn right for about 300 yards where turn right again as signposted to North Marston. This is a gated road, and it leads you over the disused railway line — more pleasing view right then left — and on to pass the gabled Hill End Farm. Some further 300 yards beyond farmhouse make another right turn on rough track marked 'Private Road'.

Rising up through the arable land it encounters a gate — 'To Farm Only'. Continue on, simply staying with curving track till it straightens out and the farm comes into sight. At this point use gate on left and walk forward, thus Farm is off to your right. We are aiming at the top of the hill, so go left and up. There are wide-spreading views over north Buckinghamshire. Nearing the summit, and on arrival at far edge of pastureland keep forward via a rickety wooden gate, found about 40 yards from right-hand corner.

Almost at once a row of windswept, somewhat desolate trees bounds your right hand, their roots splaying out above the ground. When trees end, the next gate, waymarked, ushers you forward as the radio mast topping Quainton Hill acts as an outstanding landmark. Walk towards it to go through another gate, and on, up and over hill, so that you pass the mast and triangulation station.

A well-defined track brings you straight down, through further gate and unquestionably on.

Quainton is only a short way off now, though only its tallest buildings, the church tower and the mill, thrust out above the screen of trees.

On arrival at road, just short of entrance to Ladymead Farm, go right to pass by a cattle grid and a few yards further on right again. This is Church Street returning you to The Green.

It is a road full of architectural interest. First, there is the church itself which is rich in large monuments, and then the attractive almshouses built within sight of the church by Richard Winwood in 1687, as a plaque over both porches proclaims.

Quite a number of dates appear in Quainton, as on the fine brick and flint house dated in outsize figures, 1722, while the house next door reveals that its foundations were not laid till a couple of centuries later.

Refreshments. Pubs in village.

WALK 17

WING
Waterloo Farm, Burcott.
4 Miles

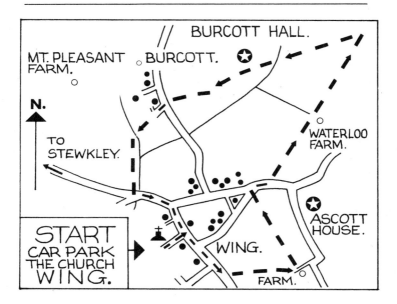

Wing Church is the village's greatest treasure, and even if it is not open, it is worth wandering up Church Street to marvel at it looking out over fields and village. Extraordinarily, much of the original Saxon work remains, including the crypt and the rough walls of the apse which have withstood the vicissitudes of over 1300 years.

The church is the setting-off point for this walk, along fieldpaths and by-ways over gently undulating countryside.

How to get there. By car — Park near church or in village.

By bus — United Counties 141, Leighton Buzzard – Wing.

From the church walk down Church Street to the High Street, where see the resplendent sign of the *Cock*. Turn right along High Street, past the *Queen's Head,* where it becomes the Aylesbury Road. The next inn you pass is the *Dove,* and then a row of almshouses given to the village by the Dormer family in the time of Elizabeth I. But as the road bends right, leave it, because our route is ahead along Park Gate.

After 70 yards go left via kissing-gate to follow P.F. Initially walk in line with fence left, with far-reaching views to the south. Then the well-defined path just asks to be followed towards the white gabled house ahead. Pass second kissing-gate on way, and when house is reached you see yet another gate by a P.F. sign, do **not** go through, but turn around to execute a 'V' turn and walk up field close to house right. On arriving at stile cross and go on, thorn hedge now right. The ground rises slightly, and the next gate, on edge of a spinney, merely escorts you round to climb a stile into further meadowland.

Forward again for 40 yards where use gate in hedgerow on right, and immediately turn left along well-trodden fieldpath. The wooded grounds seen off to right belong to Ascott House, one of the Rothschild mansions now cared for by the National Trust.

On meeting a crossing path go left for half a dozen paces only then turn right, thus staying to right of allotments. Quite quickly you will come out by gate to Leighton Road. There's a footway on opposite side, so cross with care and turn right for no more than 100 yards to climb stile on left — not the easiest I've met! Now, bear right along curve of a recently constructed roadway for further 100 yards, and again right over stile in fencing.

Once over, path tends to peter out, so walk half left over grass and under the telegraph wires. At far corner go through gate to find a tractor-track taking you straight to buildings of Waterloo Farm. On arrival at farm's concrete drive do **not** go along it, but turn left to cross the stout fence serving as a stile. Once over, maintain former direction by going half right across small, irregularly shaped meadow towards obvious wide gap in hedge.

From here on there is still little sign of the path on the ground, though your goal — the line of pylons on the horizon

— is clear enough. So keep forward in a north-easterly direction up field towards its far corner. A few yards short of corner see small gate right which go through and forward again, i.e. quickly cutting across corner of field. On reaching gate go through, or over, and veer slightly left to cut across corner of meadow to visible stile. Forward again, without changing direction, to reach and go under line of pylons.

Proceed a yard or two to stile. Instead of climbing it, turn, and with your back to it walk down right edge of same field. Follow round, soon with hedge right, till you are a few yards from far corner, where go right through gap.

Now bear half left, with white house topping the rise as your goal. At first the way dips down quite sharply and a stout plank takes you across a ditch. Once in next meadow go on uphill with red brick Burcott Hall away right, to arrive at concrete drive close to the white house. Here turn left to follow line of long drive to ultimately reach road by a rather dilapidated kissing-gate and P.F. sign.

You have arrived at Burcott. Cross over and go forward down road opposite for a few yards to discover on left a P.F. sign. Beginning as a gravel drive between houses, the path delivers you to a stile which climb into meadow. Maintain direction and when the tower of Wing Church appears left do not follow the crossing track as if towards it, but continue forward to look out for a small stile hidden in the thorn hedge.

It ushers you over stream to turn left and keep to line of hedge. The obvious single-file path wanders beside the stream till you reach road by P.F. sign. Here, by going left along road, and shortly right as signpost guides, you will return to Wing.

Refreshments. Pubs in Wing.

WALK 18

EAST CLAYDON
Middle Claydon, Rectory Farm, Sandhill.
4 Miles

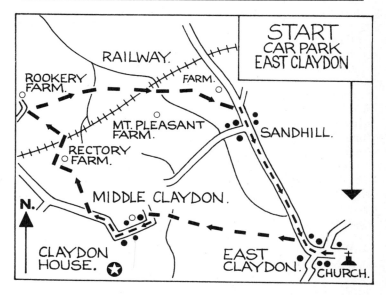

Most rewarding in early spring or late summer, this is a level walk along fieldpaths. It combines the interest of the hedgerows with plenty of opportunities for spotting rabbits and pheasants near the field boundaries, and the occasional hare racing over the open ground.

Beware of mud if wet.

How to get there. By car to park in village.

Take the 3-way road junction, marked by a venerable pollarded lime, as the starting point. Walk along road in direction of Middle Claydon and Claydon House. After about 100 yards go left, through gate to follow P.F. thus leaving behind you one of the village's several picturesque cottages. This one has a dormer set delightfully askew.

Walk straight over the grazing land passing field pond right, to reach small gate at far side. Now on with hedgerow right till next gate, waymarked, is met. Beyond, go ahead, slightly left, across large field using obvious clump of trees as your goal. When reached, still go forward but with hedge now on the left. Path is single file, and the way is soon confirmed by W.A. on an oak. On arrival at wide gap, go through towards barns and a cart track delivers you to road at Middle Claydon.

Turn left to immediately pass the small cemetery and follow road round through village. You will pass the gabled post office, and then on right a row of almshouses. From here the road dips downhill and the house and chapel of Claydon House are glimpsed away to left.

Claydon House was, and still is the home of the Verneys. Here lived Sir Edmund Verney who died at Edgehill bearing the standard of Charles I. A couple of centuries later, Florence Nightingale stayed here as a guest of her brother-in-law, Sir Harry. The house, now a National Trust property, has a simple exterior and a most lavish interior including a remarkable Chinese room.

On arrival at the lodge gates, turn right to follow P.F. over the lush meadow, going a little left and soon cross through the central avenue of oak. Make for the end of a line of trees seen left, but as you near them cross a waymarked stile just a few yards short of far corner. Some barbed wire needs to be coped with, and there is a second stile to be climbed, after which walk over field towards Rectory Farm, and on beside it till farm drive is reached.

Here a W.A. guides you right over cattle grid, and past farmyard to use metal gate. Go straight over field, bearing slightly left, to obvious white gate. This leads you to cross railway track, with appropriate care, and once similar gate and ditch have been negotiated, to arrive in field distinguished by a lone tree to right.

The way is very slightly left. The spire of Steeple Claydon's church is an unmistakable landmark, and a rare sight in Buckinghamshire. It is the largest of the Claydons, but does not happen to be on our route. So, having arrived at far boundary go over fence marked by W.A., and a further ditch to next expansive meadow. Walk across the cropped grass in the direction of clump of trees and house right; it has kennels, unseen but not unheard. For our purposes it is also just a landmark, and on meeting stile, with W.A., in far hedge leading to farm track, do **not** cross.

Instead, turn around and with your back to stile go across the same field half-left to discover wide gate ushering you into next field. Ahead here to cross stout, unmistakable stile at far side. Cross ditch by plank and on up right edge of rising field. At the top, barns appear right, and in corner of field a bridge goes over railway. Our way, however, continues a few paces left and via gap in hedge till within a short distance a kissing-gate right provides the means of crossing the railway track, close to signalman's hut.

Once through gate on other side walk half-left over small meadow, thus moving away from railway and travelling due east. Cross streamlet part way over, and then use stile/gate to enter next field. Now bear half left to far boundary where go through gate. In this field carry on without changing direction to far left-hand corner, with Ashmore Farm to left. Stiles here are not the easiest, but there is one to take you to next field, where follow hedge left for a few paces to cross another. Then in this final meadow of the walk, go forward in line with telegraph wires to emerge by way of a 2-step stile — that's a better one! — in road opposite turning to Verney Junction.

Right here as to The Claydons. Taking you all the way back to East Claydon — about 1 mile — this quiet, pleasant road has a verge for pedestrians to use. The spacious Victorian house called Sandhills is passed almost at once, and quite soon the squat tower of East Claydon will be seen.

Refreshments. Pub in village.